This book belongs to

_____

Ninja Life Hacks®
by Mary Nhin

Hi, I'm Forgetful Ninja.

It doesn't matter what I'm doing,
I can never remember things.

Why just the other day I was writing down a new recipe I had learned, but I couldn't figure out where I left my pencil.

I had tried rehearsing the alphabet backwards as fast as I could, but that just made my head hurt.

I read somewhere that if I listened to classical music, it could improve my memory.

So I attempted to listen to Beethoven in my spare time, but that didn't work.

I had even tried writing things on my notepads, but I usually forgot where I put my notepads!

Oh how I wished that I was better at remembering things.

One day, Memory Ninja stopped by.

What's for lunch?

Well, we're supposed to be having peanut butter and jelly sandwiches. All the ingredients are written in this book. But as soon as I put the book down, I forget what the ingredients are.

I have an idea to help you remember. Would you like to hear it?
Yes please.
I learned a strategy called A.A.I.

The next day, I was doing my homework.
I was studying for a school test about outer space.

I grabbed my science book. "So, the book says that the right order for the planets is Mercury, Venus, Earth, Mars, Jupiter, Saturn, Uranus and Neptune. M, V, E, M, J, S, U, and N."

NEPTUNE

JUPITER

MARS

SATURN

URANUS

EARTH

VENUS

MERCURY

SUN

Indeed. Can you think of a memorable saying that will help you remember the order?

SCIENCE

Now you have a go. Your teacher is Mrs. Steel. How will you remember her name?
She sounds like a superhero. I can see her in my head! She's holding a steel bar.
Well, there you go. Now you can remember people's names!

From that point on, I wasn't so forgetful.

I use acronyms, acrostics, and imagery or A.A.I.
(see what I did there?)

Now, I'm a forgetful ninja less often.

Remembering A.A.I. could be your
secret weapon against forgetfulness.

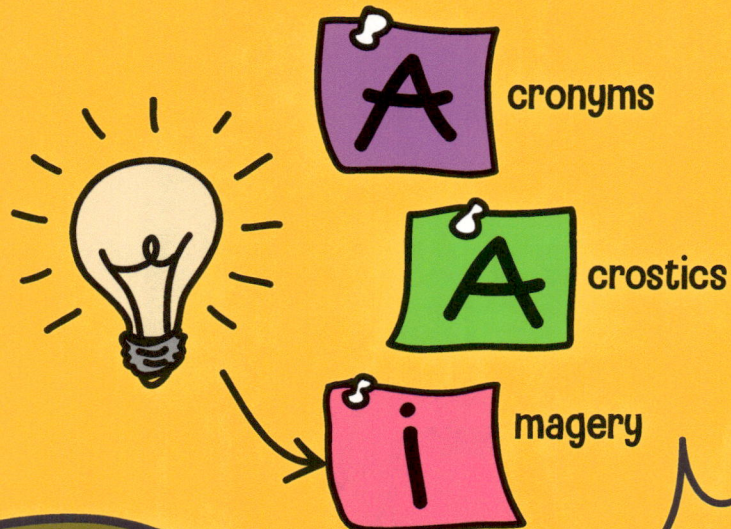

Acronyms

Acrostics

imagery

Check out the Forgetful Ninja lesson plans that contain fun activities to support the social, emotional lesson in this story at ninjalifehacks.tv!

I love to hear from my readers.
Write to me at info@ninjalifehacks.tv or send me mail at:

Mary Nhin
6608 N Western Avenue #1166
Oklahoma City, OK 73116

@officialninjalifehacks

@marynhin @officialninjalifehacks
#NinjaLifeHacks

Mary Nhin   Ninja Life Hacks

Ninja Life Hacks

www.ingramcontent.com/pod-product-compliance
Lightning Source LLC
Chambersburg PA
CBHW041241020426
42333CB00002B/39